IMAGES
of Scotland

COATBRIDGE

Best Wishes

Irene Mair

Councillor Andrew Burns, who has contributed greatly to this work. This photograph was taken in Tripoli, North Africa, in 1958.

IMAGES
of Scotland

COATBRIDGE

Helen Moir

TEMPUS

First published 2001
Copyright © Helen Moir, 2001

Tempus Publishing Limited
The Mill, Brimscombe Port,
Stroud, Gloucestershire, GL5 2QG
www.tempus-publishing.com

ISBN 0 7524 2132 8

Typesetting and origination by
Tempus Publishing Limited
Printed in Great Britain by
Midway Colour Print, Wiltshire

Contents

Acknowledgements

I would especially like to thank the following people and institutions: Fiona McNair (*Airdrie and Coatbridge Advertiser*); Mr David Wilson; Mr Bill Scott; Tom and Anne Sneden, Motherwell; Coatbridge Library; Albion Rovers Football Club; Mr Allan MacKenzie (Airdrie Library). This book could not have been accomplished without their help and contributions.

I would like to give a very special mention to Councillor Andrew Burns (Langloan and Bargeddie) for his marvellous knowledge and for his support and belief in my work. I dedicate this book to him, his lovely wife Margaret, and his family.

I would also particularly like to thank Mr John McVeigh, manager of Albion Rovers Football Club; I am grateful for his wonderful help and encouragement.

Lastly, I would like to give a special thank-you to my husband Bill for his unfailing love and support.

Introduction

The town of Coatbridge lies nine miles east of Glasgow in what was once the industrial heartland of Scotland. Coatbridge, once an accumulation of villages, became a Burgh in 1885 and is now one of the two main towns of the Monklands

Monklands District was created in 1975 upon local government re-organisation and became an autonomous district in the last re-organisation of local government. The history of the area dates back to over 3,000 years ago. Bronze Age cists were discovered on two different occasions around Drumpellier House, both containing human remains. Other evidence of early settlement has been found around the area. During the work to increase the depth of Lochend Loch in 1931-1932 a previously unknown Iron Age crannog was discovered. The crannog was a collection of buildings built on an artificial island in the loch and it is still visible today, dependent on the water level.

Roman occupation took place when Scotland was invaded. The area around here was part of the frontier zone, being just south of the Antonine Wall. The wall was built of earth and was used as a way of restricting movement and creating a buffer zone between the uncivilised parts of Scotland and the occupied area. The main Roman road to the north passed through the Monklands and further evidence of the Romans was found at Braco, near Caldercruix, when a hoard of Roman coins was discovered around 1842.

After the Roman period, the Monklands entered the Dark Ages, a period that lasted for about 500 years and of which we know very little today. While there was almost definitely Christian settlement in this period, it was not until the twelfth century that the area became known for its Christian beliefs when King Malcolm IV gave the lands formerly owned by Gillepatrice MacKerran to the monks of Newbattle in 1162. The monks belonged to the Cistercian order and were great farmers. The wool from their flocks was used in the manufacture of cloth, used for making their habits and cowls. They managed a large Grange at Drumpellier and their land became known as the 'monk lands', hence the modern day name of the district.

The monks owned mills at Gartlea, Kippsbyre, Gartmillian, Langloan and Haggs and maintained a court house or chapel near the north side of Kipps Burn. The chapel built around the middle of the fourteenth century was partially destroyed sometime during the reformation. The name of Monklands first appears in 1323 in the Steward's Charter, so named after Walter Steward, who gave the monks the right of passage through their land. Steward was the son-in-law of Robert the Bruce.

The small hamlets of Old Monkland, Kirkshaws, Langloan, Whifflet, Gartsherrie, Dundyvan, Coatbridge and Coatdyke began slowly over the centuries to merge into one cohesive settlement. In 1755 the population of Old Monkland was only 1,813 but by 1791 the records show that the population had more than doubled to 4,000. The main reason for this sudden growth was the industrial expansion of the area. From weaving to coal and ironstone mining, the industry grew to encompass iron founding and the manufacture of tools and tin plate. From the turn of the nineteenth century growth was rapid with the population growing from a few thousand to a few tens of thousands in forty years.

In 1885 the villages that composed Coatbridge came together and the town became a Burgh. On becoming a Burgh the town had to conform to clean air acts and other public health legislation. Prior to 1885 the town was the most polluted in Scotland.

The parish of Old and New Monkland played a major part in the covenanting period, with many taking part in local battles such as at Bothwell Bridge. One of the most notable local Covenanters was Robert Hamilton of Airdrie House and another, John Whitelaw of Stand, was executed in Edinburg in 1683.

While coal was known in the area in the mid fourteenth century and the monks were opencasting local outcrops, it was not until the 1790s that large-scale coal mining and iron working started to take place. David Mushet, manager of the Calder ironworks, discovered the rich ironstone called Blackband but it wasn't until the 1820s that a method of successfully converting this ore to iron was invented. When the invention of the hot blast process came along it totally revolutionised local iron founding and many works sprang up to utilise the iron rich ore.

The Monkland Canal was built to serve the local mines and rapidly became one of the most successful ventures in canal history. There was so much trade that the canal made huge profits for many years. It was surveyed and built by James Watt, the inventor and engineer

By the 1820s the Iron Horse had come to the town and Coatbridge was rapidly criss-crossed by a network of railway lines owned by different companies. By the late 1950s the canal was deemed dangerous and began to be filled in and, with the loss of much of the industry, the railway lines slowly closed as traffic dwindled.

Nowadays the town is barely recognisable from its peak as Scotland's eighth largest town. The industry that gave the town its nickname has gone, the canal has been filled in and many of the factories have been demolished. All that remains to show the town's once rich industrial past is Summerlee Heritage Park, built on the site of one of the ironworks. The museum gives just an insight into the heritage of the Burgh, but is an excellent day out for those interested in what made Coatbridge the town it is today.

One
Streets and Houses

The Whitelaw Fountain was erected in 1875 by the people of Coatbridge in honour of Alexander Whitelaw. Prior to 1872 the railways passed over this spot by means of a level crossing. Alexander Whitelaw was a director of Gartsherrie Ironworks and made the railway companies build a bridge to ease congestion in this part of town. In less than forty years the traffic to and from this and the other ironworks in the area had grown to a level that meant the old level crossing could not cope with the traffic from both railways and road. The turreted building was at one time the Tower Bar and has become the Wheeltappers & Shunters public house. The three-storey building is the Airdrie Savings Bank which was constructed in 1920 on the site of what had been the Royal Hotel.

The fountain itself has also caused traffic congestion and has moved at least twice. The Royal Hotel was constructed by the Baird brothers in 1835 and played a part in one of the cholera outbreaks in the town. The two major outbreaks in the town were in 1832 and 1848. During the later outbreak a special hospital was set up on the south side of the Monkland Canal, next to the tile and brick works. Houses were fumigated and whitewashed and tar was poured on to the streets and then set alight to purify the 'tainted' air. This was in the days before the source of cholera was understood and these precautions had little effect on the outbreaks. With many families living in squalid conditions and, with a general lack of hygiene, control of the epidemic was difficult and many doctors would meet at the Royal Hotel to hold crisis talks and meetings to discuss the epidemic.

Church Street looking from Sunnyside Station. The area has suffered greatly and most of the buildings in this view are no more. Only the bungalows at the top of the street remain – the once busy shops have been demolished.

Main Street looking towards the Cross.

Alexander Lees is still famous for its Macaroon bars and Snowballs. By the mid 1920s Alexander Lees had already built up a very large and successful business in Coatbridge. There were four grocery stores in the town at Bank Street, Main Street, Buchanan Street and Dundyvan Road as well as a confectionery at 137 Bank Street. From this beginning grew the Lees empire of today. Snowballs and Macaroon bars are now exported the world over from a factory in Calder Street. A famous jingle went: 'Lees, Lees if you please, ask for Lees on bended knees.'

Bank Street, Coatbridge.

At its industrial peak Whifflet was a very smoky place, surrounded as it was with a series of iron works and small foundries. It was said that you could walk down the street in a white shirt and by the time you got from one end to the other the shirt was black with soot. The Big Tree pub is still a local landmark.

Whifflet Street at Easton Place. This was a square of about twenty houses on the right side of the bridge. Records from the New Statistical Account of 1841 show that Whifflet had three ironstone and two coal pits even then.

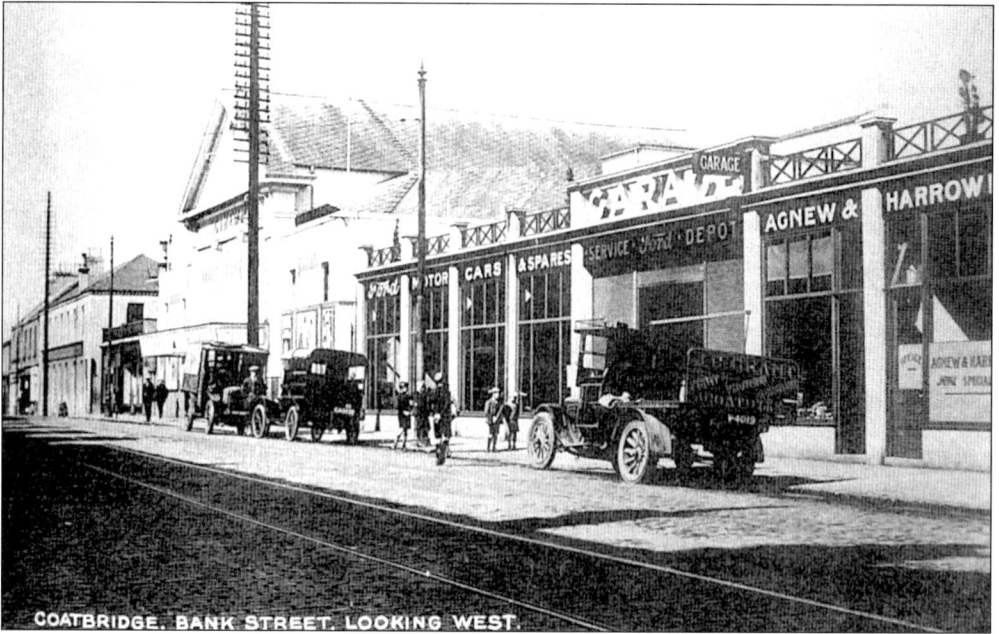

Bank Street, looking west. The Coatbridge cinema opened in 1913 which was at the peak of the early cinema boom in Britain. The cinema was the town's first purpose-built cinema. Agnew & Harrow's garage at 28 Bank Street was an agent for Ford cars (which were made at Old Trafford in Manchester).

Number 18 Bank Street has had a number of uses over the years. The two-storey red brick building was once the Poor Law offices and then became Welfare Services and then the Social Work Department. The row of shops has housed a variety of businesses including Mills & Co., who sold 78 records and sheet music.

No.30 Chrichton Street with a horse and cart belonging to A. Thomson, dairyman and cow keeper.

Main Street.

Main Street, *c*.1930

The ABC Cinema in Main Street was showing *White Christmas* and *When Eight Bells Toll* when this photo was taken.

Merrystone Bridge, looking westwards. The buildings on the left are a part of Bank Street. McIver's cabinetmakers and a doctor's surgery were just some of the businesses here. Cullen Street branched off here and the stables belonging to Rankin's dairy were located there. With the expansion of the iron industry in the 1830s a great many English ironworkers were brought to the town and houses were constructed here for them. They were built in a style that the English were accustomed to and had four apartments in their two storeys.

In the background is West End Park, Langloan. The monument is the Janet Hamilton Memorial which was erected in 1880. Janet was a famous local poet and lived in Langloan. She was the wife of a shoemaker and married at the age of thirteen. Janet began writing poetry at the age of fifty after teaching herself to write and her poetry was admired for its integrity and honesty. She died on 30 October 1873 and is buried in Old Monkland churchyard.

The Coatbridge Temperance Halls, 27-28 Sunnyside Road. The society was founded in 1832 and was probably a backlash to the number of public houses and inns in the town. The town had many pubs and a minister in the 1790s even commented on the effects of all of these drinking establishments on the local populace. In this spot in the 1860s was the Star Hotel.

The Caledonian Railway station.

Sunnyside Road with a horse and cart. Up until the 1930s horse-drawn delivery vehicles were common in all British towns as the cheapest form of haulage. Here the horse and cart are parked facing the pavement for ease while on the slope.

21

The Monkland Canal being filled in at Bank Street. This part has been culverted but the canal heading past Baillieston to Easterhouse is now under the M8 motorway. Only small bits of the canal remain visible in Coatbridge.

An aerial view of 1929 showing just how good the rail routes through the town once were. The first railway to Coatbridge was the Monkland & Kirkintilloch Railway which arrived in 1826. By the 1850s Coatbridge was criss-crossed by different lines, some owned by large concerns such as the Caley (Caledonian) railway and others by the local ironmasters and mine owners such as Bairds at Gartsherrie.

The Whitelaw fountain has been moved at least three times since it was constructed in August 1875. Each of the four basins at the bottom of the fountain once had a metal cup attached to it, secured by a chain, that locals could use. In the view above many of the buildings to the right have been demolished. The Circle Bar was given its name because of its location on the gushet site at the end of Main Street and East Canal Street.

The Theatre Royal opened in 1875 as a theatre and opera house. After eight years lying derelict the theatre (used for many variety shows in its later life) was demolished in 1966. The town's first theatre, the Adelphi, was opened in 1863.

Previous page:
The Whitelaw fountain in the 1930s with the ABC Cinema and Regal Picture House in the background.

Dunbeth Road with the Municipal Buildings on the left.

Baird Street was named after Baird of Gartsherrie, the local landowner who was responsible for developing much of Coatbridge.

The three bridges, with the bridge over the Monkland canal on the bottom right.

Dundyvan Street and Turner Street. Cairns Bar sood at the bottom of Turner Street. A common site in Coatbridge for a long time was the sheer number of pubs, often frequented by ironworkers and coal miners after work.

The Coatbridge Coat of Arms was granted by the Lord Lyon on 2 December 1930. The town's motto is 'To Labour is to Pray'.

COATBRIDGE,

Prior to 1930 the town did not have a coat of arms but a town seal which was made up of five distinct panels.

Now the site of the Time Capsule, this is Dundyvan Road and Buchanan Street with James Lynch's barbers shop and a pawnbrokers above.

Church Street, looking up from Main Street.

Another view of Church Street showing the Post Office on the left, Middle Church and at the top of the street, Gartsherrie Church.

Bank Street, Langloan, with some barefooted children following the horse and cart.

Coatbridge from the air with many local landmarks clearly visible from an unusual angle.

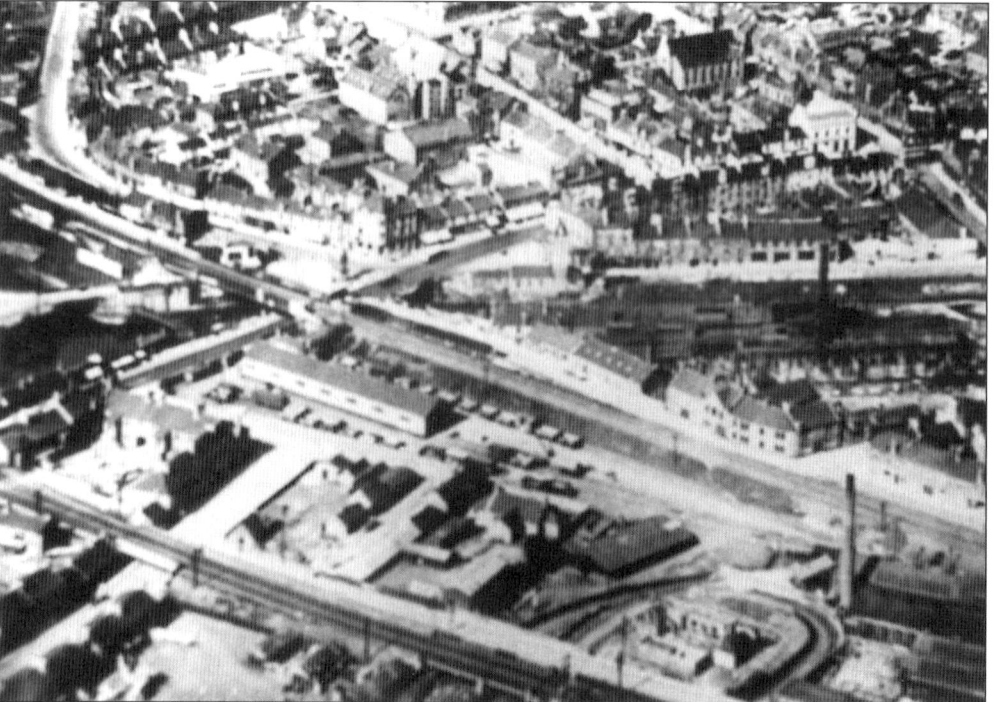

Another view of the town from the air.

Turner Street with Kate Devoy's Dairy.

Douglas Street with Robertson's which was formerly a shop called Jeanie Peacock's.

Coatdyke was one of the number of villages swallowed up by Coatbridge as it expanded to become the eighth largest town in Scotland. Originally the Cross had a small tollhouse. Here there are some roadworks and the trams are trapped at one end of the line.

Cattle are being driven along Bank Street, probably either on their way to or from market.

Just for comparison, here is a much more recent view of Bank Street showing just how much has changed along this short stretch.

Albion Street, sometime in the late 1960s.

The Hibernian Hall in Coats Street. The photos previous to this are courtesy of Councillor Andrew Burns and his wife, Margaret.

Two

Do You Recognise Anyone?

The wedding of Councillor Andrew Burns and his wife Margaret on 30 December 1961. From left to right: James Burns, Agnes Snedden Burns, Agnes Burns, Andrew Burns, Margaret McCulloch Burns, Kathleen Stevenson, Mrs Sarah Thomas, Tom McCulloch.

Whifflet Park Bowling Club, 2000, with President Mary Wilson throwing the first jack. Others on the committee are Margaret McCutcheon, Eleanor Laurieston and Moira McKendry. (Photograph courtesy of the Airdrie & Coatbridge Advertiser).

Maggie Keegans hanging out the washing on the line at back green, Barrowfield, c.1940.

The Miller family at Meadowside Cottage, Riggend, near Greengairs.

Coatbridge Bowling Club's opening for the 2000 Season. President A. Drummond looks on as his wife Mona throws the first bowl to officially open the green. Also pictured are, left to right: Vice President A. Lang, Secretary A. Baxter, Treasurer J. Corr, Secretary G. Lowe, Lanarkshire B.A. district secretary J. Reid, Monklands B.A. representative A. Kyle, Honorary President Harry Osborne, Honorary President J. Gemmell, Lady President S. Baxter and Mrs Margaret Lang. The piper is Billy Coleman (Photograph courtesy of the Airdrie & Coatbridge Advertiser).

Lang's the Butcher's on 147 High Street. The lady on the right is Kate Thomas Stevenson.

Birrel's sweetie shop was next to the Odeon Cinema. Here is Kate Thomas Stevenson again.

Langloan Primary School, 2000, with the pupils performing Pinafore Pirates as part of their Christmas celebrations. As well as Pinafore Pirates, the children also performed a story entitled Christmas Cards about aliens visiting Earth to find out about Christmas. (Photograph courtesy of the Airdrie & Coatbridge Advertiser).

The two lads in this 1950s photograph, taken outside Woolworth's in Main Street, are Johnny McLean and John McCulloch.

Councillor Andrew Burns stands outside the now-demolished Coatbridge Hotel.

Ann McGlone celebrating her award of an MBE in the Queen's Honours List of 2000. Ann has run the St Monica's Girls Club for thirty-seven years. Each week over forty girls, aged between five and twelve, attend the club and participate in a range of activities from football, drama and singing (Photograph courtesy of the Airdrie & Coatbridge Advertiser).

The staff of Dunbeth Nursery Centre celebrating the opening of their brand new premises in the education building next to St Patrick's High School. Dunbeth Nursery Centre has space for 120 children as well as a crèche for Coatbridge College students. (Photograph courtesy of the Airdrie & Coatbridge Advertiser).

Four year old Kieran Gallagher unveils the plaque to officially open the new nursery premises. (Photograph courtesy of the Airdrie & Coatbridge Advertiser).

An early horse-drawn ambulance from c.1925. The man driving the ambulance is the father of David Wilson. He was the last man to drive this ambulance and the first to drive the new motor ambulance into Coathill Hospital. This view is at Ward 2 for infectious diseases.

Two nursing sisters at Coathill with the horse, which was called Bobby.

The pupils of Townhead Primary School showing off their poetic talents at the school's Burns Competition. Here are the winners and runners up from primary one to seven, who each received a certificate for their efforts. (Photograph courtesy of the Airdrie & Coatbridge Advertiser).

Alex Miller and Mattie MacDonald Miller.

Alex Miller, a joiner and cabinet maker, who emigrated to Toronto, Canada, at his family home in Greengairs.

The Scots Guards visit Drumpark School, Bargeddie, Christmas 2000. They handed out sweets and chocolates to the kids.

A view taken at the Loch's, Coatbridge, showing Willie MacDonald, a miner at Rosehall pit, and Lizzie Keegans MacDonald.

Members of the Whifflet Burns Club celebrate their 76th anniversary in 2000.

Corsewall Street Community Centre, 1942, with a chap doing a passable Adolf Hitler impersonation. (Photograph courtesy of the Airdrie & Coatbridge Advertiser).

Three

Seats of Learning and Places of Worship

Gartsherrie Academy was built by the Baird family in 1845 to educate the children of their employees. It cost £2,000 at the time and over the years has been extended and added to. On the second floor there were fifteen classrooms arranged around a central hall. After lying derelict for a while the building is being converted into luxury flats.

St Patrick's RC School in Kildonan Street.

Dundyvan Public School.

St Mary's RC School.

The staff at St Augustine's RC School. Back row, from left to right: Mrs Malone, Mrs Curran, Mrs Vallerly, Mrs Cleary, Miss McCarroll. Middle row, left to right: Miss Collins, Miss fearnon, Miss Hagan, Mrs McConnachie, Mr James Paterson (Second Master), Mrs Corbett, Miss Kelly, Miss Ruke. Front row, left to right: Mrs McMurtagh, Mrs Burns, Miss McMullan, Mr James Austin (Schoolmaster), Mrs McBeth, Miss Diamond (schoolmistress), Mrs Kennaway,

Gartsherrie Primary School.

Bargeddie School was built in 1894 to serve the mining communities of Bargeddie, Cuilhill and Langmuir. Cuilhill and Langmuir have disappeared as have the mines they served. (Photograph courtesy of the Airdrie & Coatbridge Advertiser).

Gartsherrie Academy as it lay derelict before the current conversion to flats.

Coatbridge High School burned to the ground in 1929 and a new school was rebuilt on the site. All that remains of the original building is the janitor's house on Muiryhall Street.

Coatbridge College. (Photograph courtesy of the Airdrie & Coatbridge Advertiser).

St Francis Xavier College at Shawhead.

Old Monkland Parish Church was built in 1790 and this view of it dates from 1904. The church is on the site of a much older ecclesiastical site. In the 1850s one of the graves was opened up for a fresh internment and the body of James Merry, who had died in 1807-8, was found to be preserved perfectly and had petrified into a hard blue substance. After a few hours his body crumbled. Minerals in the water had caused the petrification and a few more bodies were found like this within the graveyard.

The entrance to Old Monkland Parish Church.

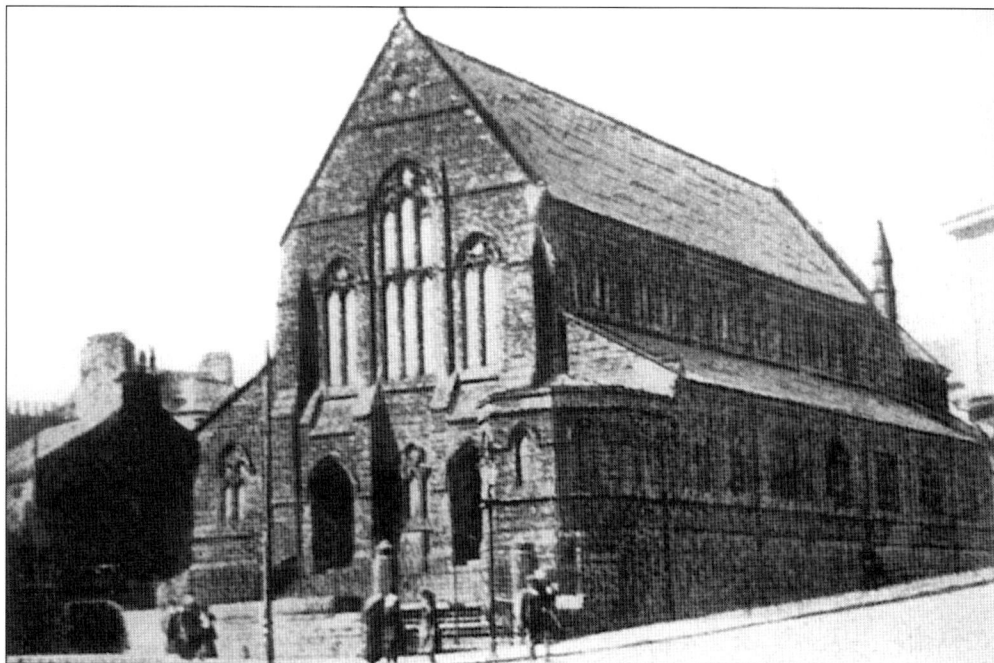

St Patrick's RC Church.

The beautiful interior of St Patrick's.

St Andrew's Parish Church.

Coats Parish Church is built on the highest spot of Coatbridge and opned in 1875.

West Free Church, Coatbridge. (Photograph courtesy of the Airdrie & Coatbridge Advertiser).

Dundyvan Parish Church. (Photograph courtesy of the Airdrie & Coatbridge Advertiser).

St Augustine's RC Church.

Buchanan Street Church. A book entitled *A Man Named Peter* was written about one of the ministers.

Another view of Old Monkland church.

St Patrick's RC Church in St John Street.

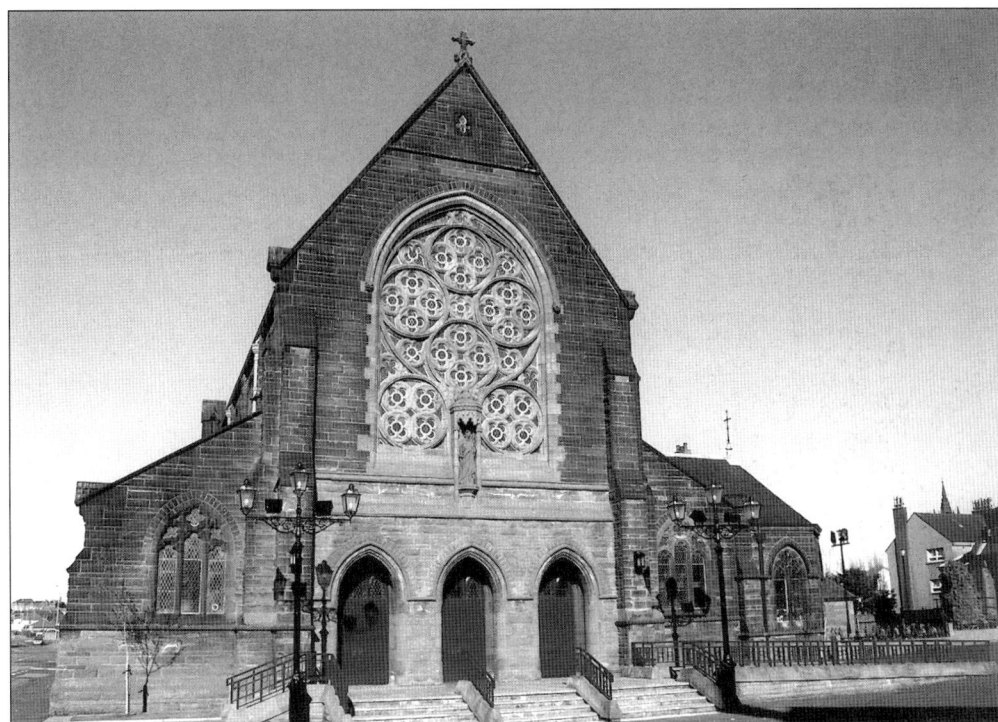

St Augustine's RC Church.

Rochsolloch Road, Coatdyke, with All Saints RC Church in the background. The congregation moved from All Saints to Holy Trinity in Muiryhall Street in 1976. The sandstone building to the right was used as a model lodging house but only the bottom floor remains today.

Four
Industry & Transport

Shawhead Pits at Whifflet. In 1790 there were four pits in the Monklands and by the 1860s there were over seventy. The abundant mineral wealth of the burgh and the area around kept the furnaces going in Coatbridge for over a century but by the 1950s everything was being worked out. Now mining of both coal and ironstone is but a distant memory.

Miners at Bedlay Colliery. Prior to nationalisation conditions for miners were often very poor and many owners provided poor housing and pay.

A mock-up of the inside of a mine showing the hazardous conditions that miners often had to work in. Men would often lie in inches of water at the coal face mining the coal. Seams were often as thin as 3ft. The sound of the mine horn was an alarming one because it often meant that there had been an accident underground. You can see this display at the Time Capsule.

Miners at the coalface c.1904.

The hutches shown here were taken along to the pit shaft and brought to the surface where the coal was often screened for size and washed before being sold on. The pit ponies were brought to the surface for a couple of weeks a year but often spent much of their time underground. There were even stables underground for them.

Miners waiting to go down the shaft for their shift. Each was given a tally before going down and they had to return it when the came back to the surface. This checking-in procedure guaranteed that no one was accidentally left down the mine at the end of a shift.

A view inside a steelworks, most probably at Motherwell, but the view must be similar to that in Gartsherrie, Langloan or Summerlee.

Another view of the inside of a Lanarkshire steelworks.

Gartsherrie Ironworks was founded by the Baird family, who were originally farmers. Their fortunes began to rise when they leased a coalfield at Rochsolloch and they moved from mining into iron making in the late 1820s. They flouted the patent of a hot blast process developed by J.B. Nielson and used this successfully at Gartsherrie. They were eventually found out and taken to court, by which time they had amassed a huge fortune and paid Nielson off. Gartsherrie lasted until 1967 when the furnaces were cooled for the last time.

Phoenix & Clifton Ironworks, 1904. The Clifton Ironworks closed down in May 1913 and was followed in August 1921 by the Phoenix works. These, and many other small iron foundries, used the raw pig iron from the large ironworks for casting and for the manufacture of tubes, shovels, other tools, and iron plate. Many works lay along the route of the Monkland Canal and the canal was used for both transport and for cooling water.

The site of Martin's Works in Dundyvan Road. Also visible is the Clock Bar.

Langloan ironworks.

Langloan Ironworks.

Gartsherrie Ironworks in its prime.

Langloan ironworks meets its end. This rubble and twisted metal is all that remained after the bulldozers demolished the ironworks.

Along with Gartsherrie, Summerlee was one of the largest of the ironworks and covered a huge area of the town. The works were owned by the Wilson family and the blast furnaces towered over fifty feet into the air. They produced pig iron, so called because when the furnace was tapped the iron was let into a row of troughs that looked like suckling pigs. By 1930 Summerlee was no more and had closed its doors for the last time. Nowadays it is the site of Scotland's noisiest museum, Summerlee Heritage Park.

Andrew Dick & Son at Greenhill. (Photograph courtesy of the Airdrie & Coatbridge Advertiser).

The entrance to Summerlee Heritage Park, which is well worth a visit. (Photograph courtesy of the Airdrie & Coatbridge Advertiser).

A barge on the Monkland Canal.

The staff at Coatbridge Central Station.

Whifflet Upper Station. Railways in the area were very confusing in that in the olden days there were many companies each competing for the rich traffic of the area. This led to the railways criss-crossing the town and the situation wasn't solved until the 1940s when all of the railways were nationalised and some consolidation could take place.

Coatbridge Central. This was the old Caley (Caledonian) station and the front part is now Pullman's Bar.

The staff at Langloan station.

Gartsherrie station.

The North British Railway station looking from across the Whitelaw Fountain.

Coatbridge Central station. (Photograph courtesy of the Airdrie & Coatbridge Advertiser).

Coatbridge Sunnyside Station. (Photograph courtesy of the Airdrie & Coatbridge Advertiser).

A tram in Main Street, looking towards St Patrick's Chapel. This is a Glasgow Corporation Coronation car no.1163. The trams first came to Coatbridge in 1904.

Coatbridge tram depot in 1953.

Airdrie and Coatbridge town councillors at the Coatbridge depot of the tramway company. This picture dates from the official opening of the tramway system when all the councillors and other important people were invited for a trial spin and refreshments. After the speeches they travelled to the terminus in Motherwell Street, Airdrie.

A tram in Main Street. The Labour Exchange is to the left and a Baxter's bus stands outside O'Donnel's public bar.

The Airdrie & Coatbridge Tramways Coy.

NOTICE

RE

ALTERATION OF FARES AND STAGES.

The public are respectfully informed that the under-mentioned Alterations in Fares and Sections will be introduced on 1st January, 1911, namely :--

SECTIONS.

Airdrie Cross will be a Section Point instead of Airdrie Station.
Biggar Road will be a Section Point instead of Knox Street.
Dunbeth Road Section Point discontinued.

FARES.

The route from **Woodside Street Terminus** to **Motherwell Street Terminus** will be divided into 13 Sections, as below :---

```
0   1   2   3   4   5   6   7   8   9   10   11   12   13
```

The fares will be as follows :---

Any 2 Consecutive Sections,	. . .	$\frac{1}{2}$d.
,, 4 ,, ,,	. . .	1d.
,, 7 ,, ,,	. . .	$1\frac{1}{2}$d.
,, 10 ,, ,,	. . .	2d.
Through Fare,	. . . . .	$2\frac{1}{2}$d.

The Fare Stages, with the above exceptions, will remain **as at** present, except that the $1\frac{1}{4}$d, $1\frac{3}{4}$d, and $2\frac{1}{4}$d Fares will be discontinued.

Tramway Depot,
Coatbridge, December, 1910.

ARCH^{D.} ROBERTSON,
General Manager.

A 1910 bulletin issued by the Airdrie & Coatbridge Tramways Co. with alterations to fares. How cheap they were!

A tram outside the Main Street depot sometime between the late 1930s and 1950s.

A tram in Langloan at the top of Mill Brae.

A view at the Whitelaw Fountain. The Monkland Canal passes under here. This is a mid-1950s view, taken just at that period when we all hadn't discovered the motor car. Here the tram is kept company by a very lonely Morris Minor. Imagine the scene today with a constant stream of traffic on the roundabout from early morning to late evening.

A decorated tram car from 1914. She's decorated as a fund raiser for the Belgian refugees who had had to flee from the Germans at the start of the First World War.

A recruiting tram car at the depot in 1915.

Staff inside the tram depot sometime at the turn of the twentieth century.

A decorated tram from 1921 with Miss Leggate at the controls.

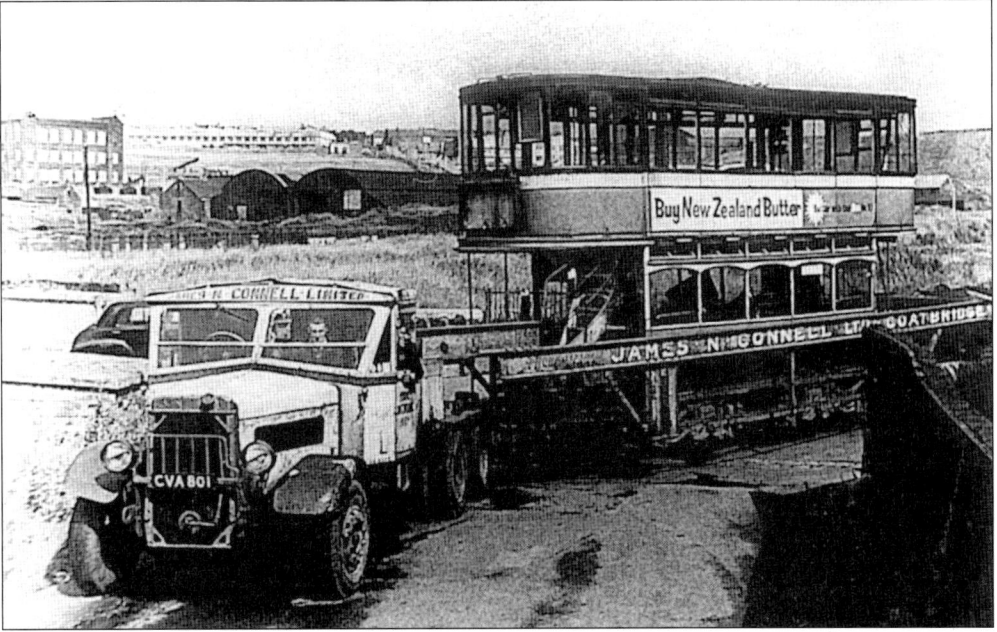

The end of an era. A tram car being removed to Connell's scrapyard in Lock Street.

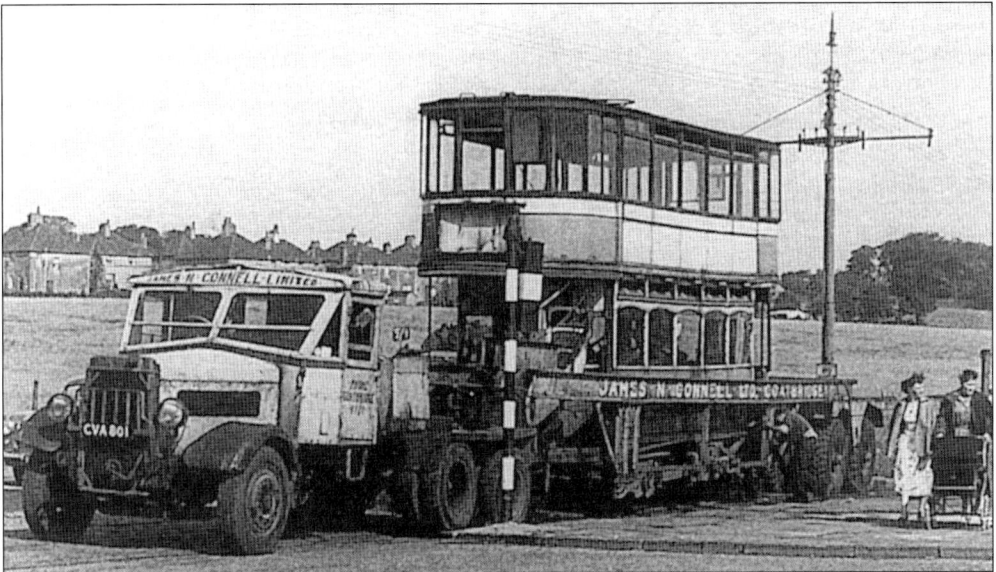

This tram car survived – here she is at Baillieston lights on her way to the Glasgow Transport Museum to be restored.

One of John Carmichael's buses from his Highland Fleet. John was a Victoria Cross holder, having been awarded his medal for placing his helmet over a grenade. When the grenade exploded he was injured but he saved the lives of countless men in his trench.

Five

A Tour Around the Town

The Cross and Sunnyside Street.

The Rob Roy Bar, Dundyvan Road.

Whifflet looking North into the town.

The canal at Summerlee. Here it is being used for leisure activities.

The Quadrant Centre.

Bank Street, Langloan, sometime about 1900. Note the bare-footed weans and the thatched roofs.

The Coatbridge War Memorial.

Many men from the town lost their lives in both world wars and are commemorated here.

Looking north to the town centre.

The village of Rosehall was once a separate settlement to the south of Whifflet Street. The miners rows that once existed there were at one time some of the worst in Britain in terms of their condition and sanitary facilities.

The Time Capsule is one of the great features of modern day Coatbridge.

Bute Terrace, Whifflet, in 1913.

Looking East from Whifflet Street.

Baird Street, with the YMCA on the left. (Photograph courtesy of the Airdrie & Coatbridge Advertiser).

Grant's shop in Main Street has now become What Everyone Wants.

Coatbridge Co-op as it once was in the Main Street.

Bank Street in the late 1960s with a learner driver filling his Morris Minor with leaded petrol.

Coatbridge Health Studio in Dunbeth Street was once the former Co-op Creamery.

Muiryhall Street, Coatdyke, with the Post Office.

Merryston Bar in Bank Street.

The Monkland Canal at Bank Street.

The Monkland Canal, looking west.

Drumpellier Country Park is an excellent place to go and relax on a summer's day.

Just to get an impression of how much Coatbridge has changed here is a modern view of the Whitelaw Fountain and Main Street. The fountain, originally placed here as a monument to the easing of traffic congestion, has become a cause of congestion itself and has been moved at least three times in its life.

The Whitelaw Fountain now resides at the side of the road, rather than as the middle of the roundabout.

Jackson Street flats before McDonalds Faraday park was constructed. (Photograph courtesy of the Airdrie & Coatbridge Advertiser).

An aerial view of the town centre with some prominent landmarks. Can you recognise the library, St Patrick's Chapel, the Police buildings, Coatbridge Baths and the Miners Rescue Services? (Photograph courtesy of the Airdrie & Coatbridge Advertiser).

Lees factory in Calder Street. Lees grew from one small shop to being one of the world's largest manufacturers of macaroon bars.

Views of the stained glass windows inside the Council Chambers.

Dating from the 1930s, this is an environmentally friendly method of moving goods round town. The Co-op van was a common sight around the town. The Co-op stables were at the corner of Jackson Street and Coats Street.

Coatbridge Library, where the staff are very helpful and informative. (Photograph courtesy of the Airdrie & Coatbridge Advertiser).

Coatbridge's Municipal Buildings at the turn of the twentieth century.

More prominent landmarks to spot from the air including St Columba High, Dundyvan Church, St Augustine's Church, West End flats, the GPO and St Augustine's primary school.

Dundyvan Road sometime in the late 1960s.

The Georgian Hotel, Lefroy Street, Blairhill.

Visible in this view are the gas works, Regal Cinema and Whitelaw Fountain.

Gartsherrie church.

Whifflet Street before the big flats were built.

Once used as Drumpellier Old Golf Club House, this is now the 1001 Air Training Coprs HQ.

The Theatre Royal on Main Street.

This part of the Monkland Canal was once known as the 'mutton hole'.

A view inside the Model Lodging House in Coats Street.

Left: Clark's Irish Supply store on the corner of Turner Street and Henderson Street. The first close on the right was known as 'Poky Mary's'. *Right:* Looking down from the slag heap to Turner Street and Henderson Street. This is now the site of Banks Social Club.

Drumpellier House was built in 1741 and was owned by the Buchanan family. Andrew Buchanan was a wealthy Glasgow tobacco merchant who amassed a huge fortune in Virginia and who spent some of his huge fortune on Drumpellier and on improving the grounds. The house was demolished in the 1960s.

Academy Street.

The town centre looking south with the Jackson high flats, Police Buildings and St Patrick's Church all visible. (Photograph courtesy of the Airdrie & Coatbridge Advertiser).

Easton Place, Whifflet.

Main Street. Galbraith's store was the former BB Picture House.

Main Street at the bottom of Academy Street.

Comparing this view with some of the other aerial shots gives an idea of how much the town centre has changed, especially with the advent of the Quadrant centre.

In August 1918 one of the new-fangled tanks came to Coatbridge on a War Bonds fund-raising exercise. This is Julian, the tank. These tanks were made at factories all over Britain, including Beardmore's at Parkhead and Dumbarton, and helped win the First World War for the Allies.

Julian is put through his paces and is shown here mounting the old walls at Cliftonhill. Tanks were excellent at travelling over the rough terrain of the Western Front battlefields.

The corner of Sunnyside Road and Main Street. On the corner is the Airdrie Savings Bank. The site was once the Royal Hotel.

A tram makes its final journey down Calder Street to Connel's scrapyard.

A back court in Dunbeth Road.

A lady bringing in the washing in a Dunbeth Road back court. In the times when all the ironworks were working it must have been impossible to dry clothes outside with all of the smoke and pollution.

Overlooking Coatbridge towards Strathclyde Country park.

Langloan, with the outdoor sports centre. Even this area has changed greatly over the years; the cinema has gone from Bank Street, the old Ford garage is no more and the canal has been filled in past Bank Street.

Coatbridge Cross in the 1920s.

The public park in Whifflet was once an oasis of green surrounded by industrial works and high density housing. In the olden days green areas like this were important. The park remains much the same today but the bowling green pavilion has been replaced by a modern building and the swings have gone. The drinking fountain erected in Coatdyke to commemorate Coatbridge's burgh status is also now in this park.

The Cinema in Bank Street, *c*.1912.

The Odeon Cinema in Main Street.

LOCH END, DRUMPELLIER PARK, COATBRIDGE.   A6300

Loch End in Drumpellier Country Park. The crannog, an ancient settlement, is visible on the left of the picture.

Coatbridge, looking west. (Photograph courtesy of the Airdrie & Coatbridge Advertiser).

The three bridges and Monkland Canal. (Photograph courtesy of William Scott, Motherwell).

Six

The Boys From The Brig

The Albion Rovers first team of 1954. When the team first moved to Cliftonhill they had their proudest moment when they reached the final of the Scottish Cup, beating Rangers in a second replay of the semi-final at Parkhead. Rovers played Kilmarnock in the final in front of 95,000 at Hampden but were beaten 3-2. In that same season they finished bottom of the league, which was a bit of a contrast. Next season they again reached the semi of the Scottish Cup, being beaten by Rangers 4-1. At that time crowds of 25,000 at club matches were not uncommon. (Photograph courtesy of John McVeigh, Albion Rovers FC).

Cliftonhill Stadium, home of Albion Rovers Football Club. The club was formed in October 1882 after a public meeting when two local clubs amalgamated. They were Albion and Rovers, hence the name. The newly-formed team played at two different locations, Cowheath (now the ASDA carpark) and the Meadow, Whifflet. They moved to the purpose built Cliftonhill stadium and it was officially opened in 1919/20. The club originally played in secondary competitions and in 1903 achieved full league status. Their first league match was against Leith Athletic in front of 2,000 supporters. They were held to a 2-2 draw at Meadow Park. (Photograph courtesy of the Airdrie & Coatbridge Advertiser).

In the 1954/55 season one of the most notable players was Phil Keirnan, whose nephew, John McVeigh is now manager of the club. In 1961 the club took the decision to change their colours from the long-standing blue to yellow and red. This was because of the number of league teams in Scotland playing in blue. (Photograph courtesy of John McVeigh, Albion Rovers FC).

Left: Another 1954 match. Many famous names are associated with the club including Jock Stein, John White, Tommy Keirnan, Danny Hegan, Tony Green and Jim Brown. These players have all been capped for their country. *Right:* In 1995 a boardroom shuffle led to a complete overhaul of the club and a number of improvements were made to Cliftonhill. Included among the improvements was the installation of new floodlights. Andrew Dick, the chairman at the time, and his colleagues were responsible for many of the improvements. Home-grown talent has been important to the club for a little while and there is a vigorous training programme for the team which has thirty-three full time professional players on its books. Here is a match of 1954 vintage. (Both photographs courtesy of John McVeigh, Albion Rovers FC).

On 22 August 1949 a severe fire destroyed the west wing of the grandstand. This was the biggest fire in the history of the town since the early 1940s when the Middle Church was destroyed. Surprisingly, the debris was cleared away in time for the Sunday fixture against Stenhousemuir to be played. This resulted in a 2-2 draw. Here is the ground in 1954, only six years after the fire. (Photograph courtesy of John McVeigh, Albion Rovers FC).

As well as being the premier football venue in Coatbridge, Cliftonhill has also been used for greyhound racing and speedway. Greyhound racing first took place in December 1931 and a speedway licence was applied for in 1950. While greyhound racing stopped in the mid-1950s, the sport of speedway took off in 1968 with the first meeting in April that year. Speedway stopped in 1977 when greyhound racing was re-introduced. Another 1954 season match. (Photograph courtesy of John McVeigh, Albion Rovers FC).

Albion Rovers play their hearts out in 1954. (Photograph courtesy of John McVeigh, Albion Rovers FC).

The first team of 1949/1950 with a few famous names in Scottish football present. From left to right, standing: Alan Muir, Bobby Kerr, Jock Stein, Andy Sinclair, Willy Black, Sam English. Left to right, kneeling: Willie Dickson, Willie Jack, Jim Boyd, Johnny Craig., Jimmy Smith. (photograph courtesy John McVeigh, Albion Rovers FC)

Albion Rovers Football Team, 1999/2000. Back row, left to right: J. McKenzie, J. McLees, I. Diack. C. Silvestro, R McMullan, I. Rankin, K. McBride. Centre, left to right: J. Lindsay (youth coach), S. Clark, B. Clyde, J. Shearer, T. Lumsden (Captain), C. Fahey, I. Harty, T. Tait, D.Young (Physio). Front Row, left to right: C. Waldie, Y. Begue, John McVeigh (Manager), A. Booth, J. Smith.